D1583163

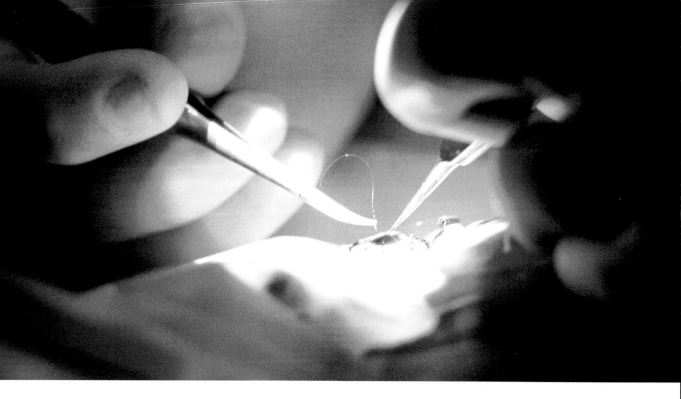

CUTTING EDGE MEDICINE

Organ Transplantation

Carol Ballard

FRANKLIN WATTS
LONDON•SYDNEY

First published in 2007 by
Franklin Watts
338 Euston Road
London NW1 3BH

Franklin Watts Australia
Hachette Children's Books
Level 17/207 Kent St, Sydney, NSW 2000

Produced by Arcturus Publishing Limited
26/27 Bickels Yard, 151–153 Bermondsey Street
London SE1 3HA

Editor: Alex Woolf
Designer: Nick Phipps
Consultant: Dr Eleanor Clarke

Picture credits:
Getty Images: 10.
Rex: 16 (TXM), 22 (Action Press), 37 (JCY).
Science Photo Library: 5 (J. L. Martra, Publiphoto Diffusion), 6 (Mike Devlin), 8, 12 (Deep
Light Productions), 15 (Kevin Beebe/Custom Medical Stock Photo), 19 (Mauro Fermariello),
21 (National Cancer Institute), 25 (Ed Young), 26 (Will and Deni McIntyre), 29 (BSIP Vem),
30 (Mauro Fermariello), 32 (Michelle del Guercio), 35 (Antonia Reeve), 38 (J.L. Martra,
Publiphoto Diffusion), 40 (BSIP, Platriez), 43 (Maximillian Stock Ltd), 44 (A.J. Photo/Hop
Americain), 46 (Science Source), 48 (Klaus Guldbrandsen), 51 (Dr Rob Stepney), 53 (Peter
Menzel), 55 (Dr Gary Gaugler), 57 (Dr Klaus Boller), 58 (Steve Gschmeissner).

Every attempt has been made to clear copyright. Should there be any inadvertent omission,
please apply to the publisher for rectification.

A CIP catalogue record for this book is available from the British Library.

Dewey Decimal Classification Number: 618.1' 780599

ISBN: 978 0 7496 6972 0

Printed in China

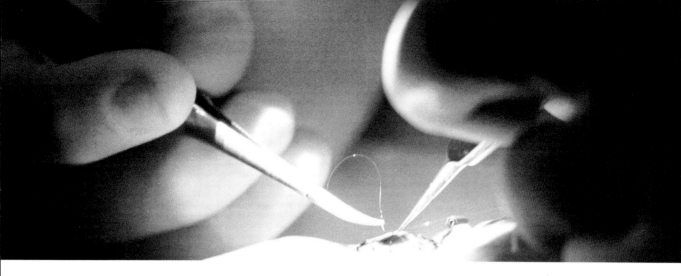

Contents

CHAPTER 1

What is Organ Transplantation?

What can be done if an important part of a person's body is unable to work properly? In many cases, taking medicines or having an operation can solve the problem. In some cases, though, the problem is too serious to be solved in these ways. The only option may be to replace the faulty part with one that does work properly. For example, the heart must pump blood efficiently around the body. If it cannot do this, a person will become very ill. By removing the faulty heart and replacing it with a healthy heart, normal blood circulation can be restored and the person can regain their health. This is called a heart transplant.

It is not just hearts that can be transplanted. Other parts of the body, such as skin, livers and kidneys can be transplanted too. Transplant operations are complex surgical procedures, requiring large teams of surgeons and other medical staff, together with

CUTTING EDGE   SCIENCE

Body organization
Like all living things, the human body is made up from millions of tiny units called cells. Cells that have a similar structure and function are grouped together to make tissues. Tissues are grouped together to make organs, which are collections of tissues that perform a specific function. Organs that carry out similar or connected functions are grouped together to make systems. For example, lots of muscle cells make up muscle tissue. Muscle tissue, together with other tissues make up the organ called the heart. The heart and other organs, such as blood vessels, together make up the circulatory system.

sophisticated equipment. Thousands of transplant operations are carried out every year.

When is organ transplantation necessary?

A transplant may be needed for several reasons, including:

- a baby born with a vital organ or organs that are not properly developed, and the defects cannot be corrected by other surgery;
- an organ irreversibly damaged by disease that cannot be treated by medicines or other surgery;
- an organ damaged as the result of an accident with damage too serious or extensive to be repaired by another means.

A transplant operation is not always a suitable solution for a patient with a failing organ. In most cases, a transplant candidate must still be physically capable of withstanding the stress of undergoing general anaesthesia, as well as the surgery itself. A lengthy recovery period often follows and may involve a number of strong medications taken for life. Any patient who is too frail and weak from age or illness seldom receives a major organ transplant.

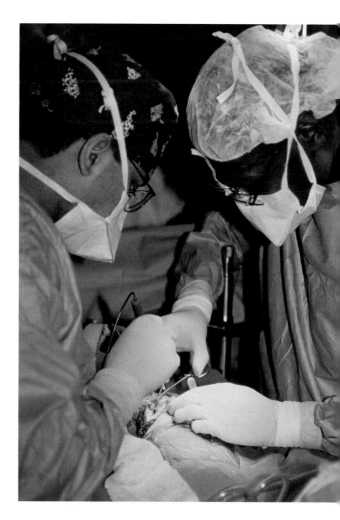

These surgeons are carrying out a liver transplant operation. A liver transplant is necessary if a patient is suffering severe liver disease and liver failure.

Types of organ transplant

There are four main types of organ transplant. Each is known as a 'graft', which means joining together. The four types of transplant are called autograft, syngeneic graft, homograft and heterograft.

Autograft This is a transplant using a patient's own tissue. *Autograft* comes from the Greek word *autos*, which means 'self'. Another name for this type of transplant is 'isograft', from the Greek word *isos*, which means 'equal'.

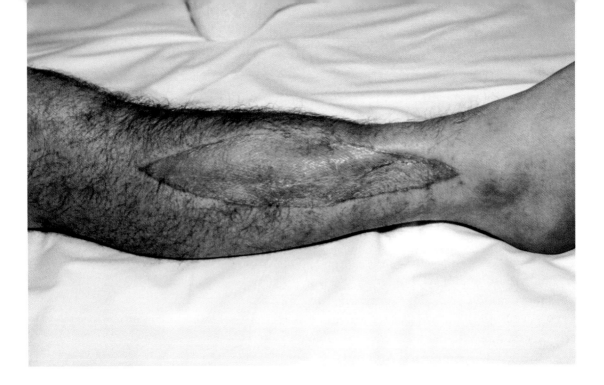

The slightly darker, elliptical patch on this man's leg is a skin graft that is healing well.

Autografts often play a major part in the treatment of patients with serious skin damage – for example, after a burn or some forms of surgery. If an area of skin is so badly damaged that it cannot repair itself, skin tissue may be taken from another part of the patient's body. This is then used to repair the damaged area. Because the body is able to repair itself, the area from which the tissue was taken will soon heal.

Syngeneic graft This is a transplant using an organ from a genetically identical individual. This can only be the transplant of an organ from one identical twin to the other, as no other people have identical genes. 'Syngeneic' comes from the Greek word *syngeneia*, which means 'kinship'.

Homograft This is a transplant using an organ from an unrelated person. Many common transplants, such as heart transplants, kidney transplants and blood transfusions are homografts. 'Homograft' comes from the Greek word *homos*, which means 'same' (that is, from the same species). Another name for this type of transplant is 'allograft', from the Greek word *allos*, which means 'the other of two'.

Heterograft This is a transplant using an organ from an individual of a different species such as a cow or a pig. An example of a heterograft is transplanting a heart valve from a cow or pig into a human, which is a common treatment for some types of heart disease. 'Heterograft' comes from the Greek word *heteros*, which means 'the other of many'. Another name for this type of transplant is *xenograft*, or *xenotransplant*, from the Greek word *xenos*, which means 'foreign'.

Early history

The history of organ transplantation goes back thousands of years. However, there is little evidence to suggest that – except for some autografts, such as skin (see page 8) – any of the early attempts were successful. Transplanting organs requires an extensive knowledge and understanding of the human body, as well as sophisticated surgical techniques. It was not until the twentieth century, when there were major advances in all branches of science and medicine, that these were developed and organ transplantation could be successfully carried out.

CUTTING EDGE   MOMENTS

Transplant milestones
Scientists have made a lot of progress since the early attempts at organ transplantation. This table shows just some of the many historic achievements in this branch of medicine.

year	place	organs transplanted
1906	Olmutz, Moravia (Czech Republic)	cornea (clear layer at front of eye)
1954	Boston, Massachusetts, USA	kidney
1956	Cooperstown, New York, USA	bone marrow (part of bone involved in blood cell production)
1963	Denver, Colorado, USA	liver
1967	Cape Town, South Africa	heart
1981	Stanford, California, USA	combined heart and lung
1986	Toronto, Ontario, Canada	double lung
1998	Cleveland, Ohio, USA	total larynx (voice box)
1998	Lyon, France	hand
2005	Amiens, France	partial face

This illustration, by the 16th-century doctor Gaspare Tagliacozzi, shows a method for repairing the lip using skin from the arm.

One of the earliest reports of a successful autograft appears in a work called *Samhita*, which was written in Ancient India and which many historians believe to be more than two thousand years old. In it, the writer, Sushruta, describes a method for using skin grafts from the cheek to reconstruct noses and ear lobes. Sushruta also described using a forehead flap and other skin grafts to repair disfigured noses. Accounts of similar autografts appear in several medieval texts.

Corneal transplants are the first homografts known to have been successful. The first documented case was reported in 1905 by Dr Eduard Zirm in Olmutz, Moravia (which is now part of the Czech

Republic). The cornea was from an 11-year-old boy and the person who received the cornea was an adult labourer blinded by a strong chemical. The man regained the sight in one eye.

The cornea is the transparent layer that covers the front of the eye. Because no blood vessels are involved, corneal transplant surgery is a fairly simple procedure, usually performed on an outpatient basis. Also, the white blood cells that make up part of the body's immune system, and which would recognize the new cornea as 'foreign' material, do not come into contact with the transplanted organ.

Breakthroughs

This highlights the two main challenges facing the early transplant surgeons. Firstly, how could they join the patient's blood vessels to those of the transplanted organ? This was crucial, because without an efficient blood supply the organ would quickly die. Secondly, how could they prevent the patient's body reacting against (rejecting) the transplanted organ? Scientists knew that this often happened, but as they did not understand how or why rejection occurred they were unable to prevent it.

A technique for joining major blood vessels was pioneered in 1902 by Alexis Carrel, a French surgeon working at the Rockefeller Institute, New York City, USA. Large blood vessels, called arteries and veins, are hollow tubes with walls made up from several layers. Carrel found that if he folded back the ends of each blood vessel like a cuff, he could stitch the inside walls together. This prevented blood touching any other tissue. He also put a special gel on his needles and threads to help prevent blood clotting. This technique was valuable to many areas of surgery and Carrel was awarded the Nobel Prize for Medicine in 1912. His method paved the way for transplant surgery.

CUTTING EDGE MOMENTS

Surgery and embroidery

Alexis Carrel became interested in finding a technique for joining blood vessels after the assassination of the French president by a knife wound in 1894. If surgeons had been able to join the president's severed blood vessels together, his life may have been saved. Carrel went to an embroiderer in Lyon, France, to learn to sew with fine needles and thread. He practised his stitching on paper until he could produce very fine, even stitches that did not go right through to the other side. Only then was he ready to try his sewing technique out on blood vessels.

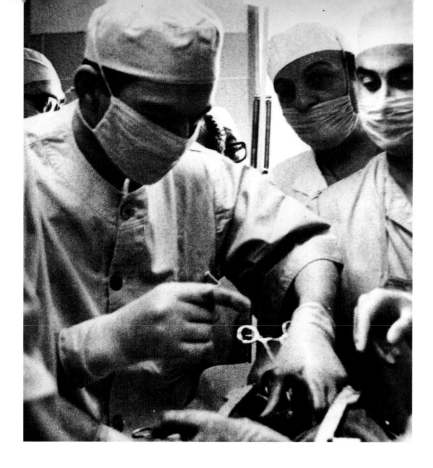

South African surgeon, Dr Christiaan Barnard, demonstrates his heart transplant methods on a dog.

The problem of rejection was solved in two main stages. The first breakthrough came in 1909 when an Austrian doctor, Karl Landsteiner, worked out the major human ABO blood group system. His work showed that there were differences between the blood of different individuals, and that blood could be put into one of four main groups, which he called A, B, AB and O. Landsteiner demonstrated that reactions that could kill a patient occur when blood from one group is mixed with blood from a different group. This meant that, for a transplant to be successful, the patient and the organ donor must share the same blood group. This was an important step towards understanding why some transplants failed. Landsteiner was awarded the Nobel Prize for Medicine in 1930 in recognition of the importance of his work.

It was not until scientists began to understand how the immune system worked that the mystery of transplant rejection was unravelled further. The immune system is the body's main defence mechanism. It includes white blood cells, parts of the bone marrow, lymph nodes and organs such as the thymus and spleen. The immune system's job is to detect and remove microbes and anything else that is not part of the body, which it recognizes as 'foreign'.

In 1944, a British scientist, Peter Medawar, discovered that animal embryos (offspring in the early stages of development) do not reject foreign tissue transplants. At the same time, an Australian scientist, Frank Macfarlane Burnet, showed that the body's immune system learns at a very early stage in its development to recognize 'self' from 'non-self', or foreign tissues. It is only later in the immune system's development that it treats things that it meets as foreign, and attacks them. Medawar and Burnet were awarded the Nobel Prize for Medicine in 1960. From their work, studying how the earliest stages of the immune system developed, scientists had a much clearer idea of how the transplant rejection process worked. They worked out that, when a patient's white blood cells meet the transplanted tissue, they recognize proteins on its cell surfaces as foreign. The white blood cells then stimulate other blood cells to attack and destroy the foreign tissue.

CUTTING EDGE MOMENTS

The first successful heart transplant

The first successful heart transplant was carried out at Groote Schuur Hospital, Cape Town, South Africa, on 3 December 1967 by the surgeon Christiaan Neethling Barnard. The patient, a 55-year-old grocer called Louis Washkansky, received the heart of a road accident victim. Washkansky survived for 18 days after the operation, but then died of pneumonia. This may not seem very long now, when patient survival times are counted in years rather than days, but at the time it was a truly astonishing achievement. In the days after the operation the whole world watched and waited to see what would happen.

Improving survival times

Since the first organ transplants were carried out, the advances in the field have led to a considerable improvement in patient survival times. Today, many kidneys still function more than ten years after transplant. More than three-quarters of heart transplant patients survive for at least five years. Doctors and scientists hope that, with further developments in areas such as surgical technique and understanding of the immune system, future transplant patients will enjoy even longer survival periods.

CHAPTER 2

Which Organs can be Transplanted?

When people hear about or talk about organ transplants, the organs that first spring to mind are often hearts and kidneys. However, many other body parts can also be transplanted. We can think of them in two main groups. The first group is solid organs and the second group is tissues, cells and fluids.

Solid organs that can be transplanted include those that lie in the chest, such as heart and lungs. They also include some abdominal organs such as pancreas, liver, kidney and intestine. In

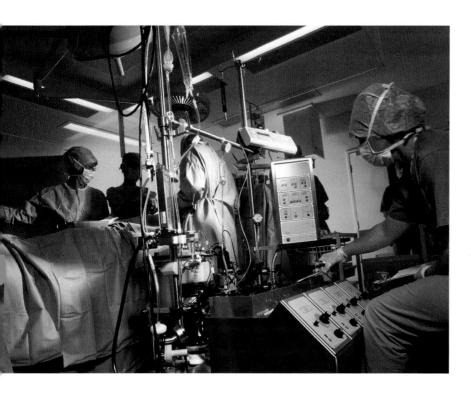

Heart-lung machines, like the one seen at the front right in this picture, allow surgeons to perform heart surgery that would otherwise be impossible.

recent years, techniques for transplanting other body parts such as hands and faces have also been developed.

Heart and lung transplants

The heart carries out the vital process of pumping blood around the body. If this process stops, a person will die within minutes. The need to keep the blood circulating posed a problem for surgeons who wanted to carry out any kind of heart operation. How could patients be kept alive while their heart was undergoing surgery? And, even worse, how could patients be kept alive while their heart was completely removed during a transplant operation? Without a solution to these problems, complex heart surgery and transplants were impossible.

An answer was provided in 1953 by John Gibbon, an American surgeon. After more than twenty years of research, he managed to develop a workable 'heart-lung machine'. This could take over the tasks of pumping a patient's blood (the heart function) and of replacing waste carbon dioxide in the blood with oxygen (the lung function) during surgery. By connecting a patient's blood supply to the heart-lung machine, surgeons could operate on the patient's heart without affecting the blood circulation. This technical development also made heart transplants theoretically possible – using this machine, a patient could be kept alive while his or her heart was removed and another put in its place.

CUTTING EDGE MOMENTS

Multiple organ transplants

On 22 March 1997, an eight-month-old Italian girl called Eugenia Borgo received seven abdominal organs. Doctors monitored her very closely and she recovered well. On 31 January 2004, a six-month-old Italian girl called Alessia di Matteo became the first person to receive eight new abdominal organs. She suffered from a digestive system disorder from which she would soon have died. At the Jackson Memorial Hospital in Miami, Florida, USA, doctors transplanted a liver, stomach, pancreas, small intestine, large intestine, spleen and kidneys into Alessia. The donor was a baby boy who had died from a heart disorder. Unfortunately, Alessia remained unwell and she died on 12 January 2005.

The heart-lung machine also made lung transplants possible. Using this machine, circulation of the patient's blood and the exchange of oxygen and carbon dioxide can be maintained while a whole lung or part of a lung is removed. A healthy lung or part of a lung can then be put in its place and the patient's normal circulation resumed. In some patients, heart and lungs are transplanted at the same time. These operations are known as combined heart and lung transplants.

Transplanting abdominal organs

The liver carries out many essential functions within the body, such as breaking down toxins, storing fats, producing blood-clotting factors and helping to break down old blood cells. However, if the liver becomes damaged or diseased its function may be impaired and a liver transplant may be necessary. All or part of a liver may be transplanted.

All the solid organ transplants discussed so far involve removing all or part of a patient's sick organ and putting a new one in its place. Kidney transplants are different, though. The kidneys filter the blood, removing waste chemicals and excess water to form urine, and ensuring the correct balance of salts is maintained. If the only problem is the failure of the kidneys to clean the blood efficiently, the patient's kidneys are left in place. A healthy kidney

CUTTING EDGE SCIENTISTS

Joseph E. Murray

Joseph E. Murray was born on 1 April 1919 in Milford, Massachusetts, USA, and studied medicine at Harvard Medical School. While practising as an army doctor at a hospital in Pennsylvania, Joseph became intrigued by tissue and organ transplantation. Through contact with Sir Peter Medawar (see page 11), Joseph developed his work on transplantation techniques and, on 23 December 1954, he carried out the first kidney transplant at Peter Bent Brigham Hospital in Boston, Massachusetts. Following this achievement, Joseph spent the rest of his working life in the field of transplantation medicine. In recognition of the importance of his work on transplantation, Joseph Murray was awarded one half share of the Nobel Prize for Medicine in 1990.

is transplanted into the patient's body, usually above the pelvic bones around where a front trouser pocket would be. However, in cases such as when a patient has cancer of the kidney, the patient's kidneys are removed, too.

Another organ that is sometimes transplanted is the pancreas. The pancreas produces insulin, which is essential for controlling the amount of sugar in the blood. If a person's pancreas does not function properly, there may not be enough insulin to control his or her blood sugar levels. People with this condition are said to be diabetic. One solution to this may be a pancreas transplant. As with kidney transplants, a patient's own organ is left in place when a pancreas transplant is carried out. The new pancreas is transplanted into the lower abdomen.

If a patient who is diabetic also has kidney failure, a pancreas and kidney transplant may be carried out together, with both new organs being put into the lower abdomen. For some diabetics, an alternative to a complete pancreas transplant is the transplantation of 'islets of Langerhans'. These are small groups of pancreatic cells that produce insulin. They are injected into the patient's liver where they settle and are able to function as they normally would in the pancreas. Scientists are developing ways of coating these cells to 'hide' them so that the patient's white blood cells do not detect them and reject them as 'foreign'.

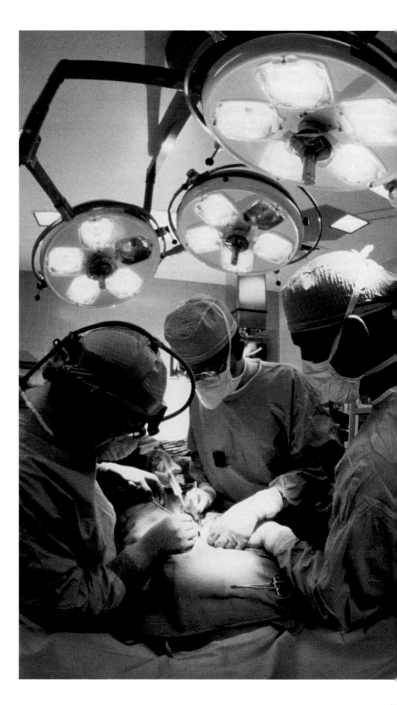

Surgeons carry out a kidney transplant operation.

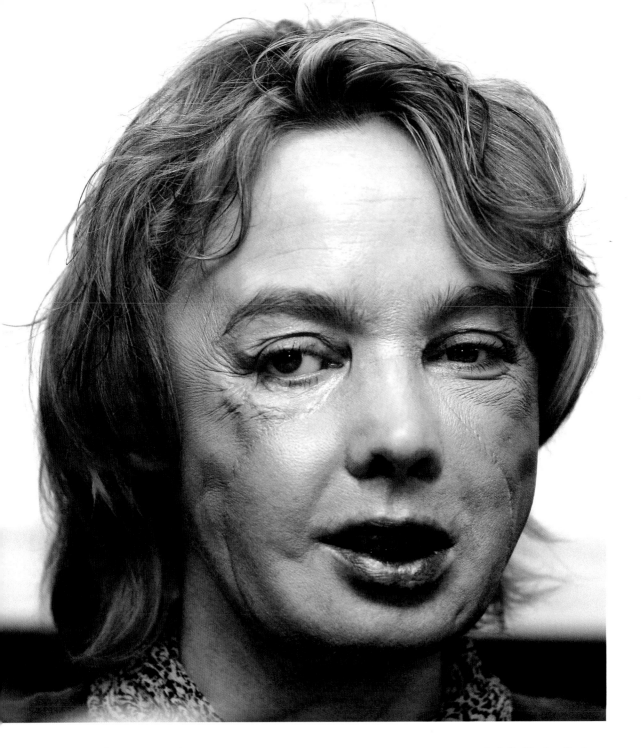

Transplanting body parts

In recent years, surgeons have begun to develop techniques for transplanting various other parts of the body.

Hand In 1998, in Lyon, France, surgeon Jean-Michel Dubernard transplanted a hand onto the arm of Clint Hallam, a New Zealander

Isabelle Dinoire after her pioneering partial face transplant. The photo was taken about ten weeks after the operation. Scars are visible where old and new facial tissue meet.

whose own hand had been ripped off in an accident involving a circular saw. The surgery was successful but Clint did not take all the medication prescribed and the transplant was later removed.

Tongue The first human tongue transplant was successfully carried out in Vienna, Austria, in 2003 when a 42-year-old man suffering from cancer of the tongue and jaw received a tongue from a dead donor.

Forearm and hand Also in 2003, the first double forearm and hand transplant was carried out at the Innsbruck University Clinic, Austria. The recipient was a 41-year-old man, Franz Jamnig, who had lost both his arms in an accident at work. The operation was successful and allowed Franz to live a more independent life again.

Partial face In 2005, surgeons in Amiens, France transplanted a nose, lips and chin to replace part of the face of a woman whose own face had been badly damaged in a dog attack (see panel).

Thumb The technique for a thumb transplant is relatively well-established. Without a thumb, a person's hand function is severely limited. It can be difficult to pick things up, grip things and hold a pen or other tool. In cases where a thumb is lost, perhaps as a result of an industrial accident, surgeons have developed a technique for replacing the thumb with one of the patient's own big toes. Although the toe may be a little bigger than the lost thumb, it can function as well and much of the patient's hand function is restored. Losing the toe has little effect on the patient's ability to walk, but may affect his or her balance.

CUTTING EDGE — FACTS

The first partial face transplant

The first partial face transplant was carried out in Amiens, France, on 27 November 2005. Isabelle Dinoire, a 38-year-old woman, had been attacked by her dog. Her nose and mouth were ripped off and, in addition to destroying her features, it left her unable to chew or speak. Surgeons removed skin and muscles from the equivalent parts of the face of a woman who had died. During a fifteen-hour operation, they transplanted the face parts onto Isabelle's face. The operation was successful, leaving her with a minimum amount of scar tissue.

The new face did not look exactly like that of the donor, as the underlying bone structure of the two women was different. Nor did the new face look exactly like Isabelle's old face, because there were differences between the two women's skin and muscles. Following the surgery, Isabelle had to learn to accept her new appearance.

Transplanting tissues

Tissues that can be transplanted include bone, skin, cornea, tendons, ligaments, arteries, veins and heart valves. More than 750,000 tissue transplants are carried out each year in the USA. Corneal transplants are more common than any other tissue or solid organ transplant. Corneas and heart valves can only be obtained from deceased donors. The other tissues may be autografts, being removed from one part of a person's body to repair damage to another part. They may also be obtained from living or dead donors.

Skin can be cryopreserved (preserved by freezing) for up to four weeks for treatment of burns victims, and longer for other procedures. For some surgery, such as periodontal work (surgery on the tissues that surround the neck and root of a tooth), skin can be freeze-dried and stored for up to five years. Skin cells can be grown over a mesh in a laboratory, to increase the area of damage that it can cover. Skin can also be stretched by inserting an expanding balloon under it before it is removed for transplantation. The balloon is filled with saline (salt) solution, and more is gradually added as the skin stretches. It is left under the skin for several weeks or months, the length of time depending on the size of new skin required.

Bone tissue can be transplanted, either as small fragments to stimulate a patient's own bone to produce new bone tissue or as larger fragments to replace pieces of damaged bone. Bone tissue

CUTTING EDGE   SCIENCE

Burns and skin grafts

The most common use of skin grafts is in the treatment of burns. The outer layer of the skin, which is made up from dead cells, is regularly worn away. Below this is a layer of living cells that divide to produce new cells, replacing those that are worn away. Below this is living tissue that contains blood vessels, nerve endings, sweat glands and other structures. A minor burn may simply damage the dead outer layer, leaving the cells below able to divide and repair the damage. In a more severe burn, the layers below are also damaged and the skin cannot repair itself. This is when a skin graft can help, providing a new outer layer to protect the body from moisture loss and infection.

Donated bone tissue can be ground up, frozen and stored until it is needed for a transplant. Bone tissue is often used to replace diseased bone or to fill in spaces around a joint replacement. Donated bone is carefully screened to ensure it is healthy.

can be used fresh within twenty-four hours of harvesting or cryopreserved for up to five years. Tendons, cartilage and ligaments can be transplanted to repair damage to joints resulting from injury or disease.

Blood vessel transplants are required during a coronary bypass operation, an operation in which a new blood vessel is grafted onto the heart to replace a blocked coronary artery. Coronary blood vessels supply blood to the heart muscle. They can become blocked, often as a result of fatty deposits. An artery from elsewhere in the body, such as the leg, arm, chest or abdomen, is used to bypass the blocked coronary artery and restore an adequate blood supply to the heart muscle.

Transplanting cells and fluids

Cells that can be transplanted include blood cells (for example, white blood cells or platelets) and bone marrow cells. Sometimes, patients require blood transfusions. A blood transfusion involves giving a patient complete blood, including plasma and all the blood cells.

Blood cells For a few days before the donation of blood cells, the donor may receive injections of drugs to increase the number of blood cells. The blood is taken from the donor at a blood transfusion centre, from a vein in the arm. The blood is passed through a machine that separates the blood cells from the rest of the blood (see panel). The cells are stored ready for transplanting and the rest of the blood is pumped back into the donor.

The storage of whole blood and separated parts of blood is carefully monitored. Whole blood can be used fresh for up to 21 days after collection. Plasma is usually frozen and used within one year. Platelets must be used within five days of donation.

Blood transfusions Although we may not think of a blood transfusion as a transplant, that is exactly what it is. Blood from a donor is stored and transplanted into another person who needs it. Blood may be needed for many different reasons, such as to replace blood that has been lost during surgery or as a result of an accident. Blood transfusions are carried out every day all around the world.

CUTTING EDGE SCIENCE

What is blood made of?

There are several different components of blood. Red blood cells transport oxygen around the body and give blood its red colour. Red blood cells are so small that it would take more than 120 to make a line 1 mm long! White blood cells are involved in defending the body against germs and disease. Most are larger than red blood cells. Platelets are tiny fragments of cells. They play an important part in helping blood to clot after a cut or other injury. The liquid part of blood is called plasma. It is clear and watery and is a pale straw colour. Many dissolved salts and other chemicals are transported around the body in the plasma.

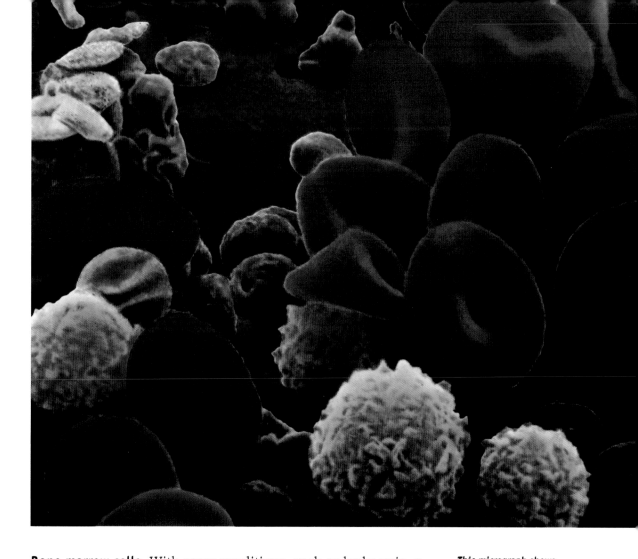

Bone marrow cells With some conditions, such as leukaemia, a person's white blood cells are diseased and not able to function properly. Because bone marrow plays an important part in the development of white blood cells, such conditions can often be cured by a bone marrow transplant, which replaces the diseased white blood cells with healthy ones. Donating bone marrow is a more complex procedure than donating blood because the bone marrow is only found within the hip bones (pelvis), skull, breastbone (sternum), ribs and thigh bones (femurs). The most commonly used source of bone marrow is the pelvis.

Donors are given a general anaesthetic (a drug that causes them to lose consciousness), so they do not feel any pain. While the donor is asleep, liquid bone marrow is removed from his or her pelvis using a special hollow needle. This can then be transplanted into a patient whose own bone marrow is unable to produce normal blood cells.

This micrograph shows human red blood cells (red discs), white blood cells (yellow) and platelets (pink).

Sources of Organs

Developing the techniques for successful organ transplants is one thing – but where do the organs that are transplanted come from? This chapter looks at the different sources of organs for transplantation. There are three main sources of organs for transplantation. These are:

1. **Living donors.** These can include the patient, someone related to the patient, someone unrelated to the patient, or another transplant patient.
2. **People who have died.**
3. **Other sources.** These can include animals, artificial organs or newly grown organs.

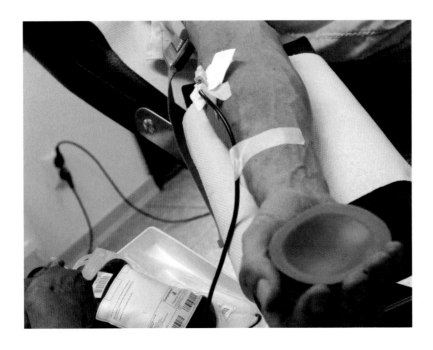

A donor gives blood. Blood can be collected via a needle inserted into a vein in the arm. The donor occasionally squeezes the blue rubber disk to help increase the blood flow to the arm, decreasing the time it takes to fill the bag with blood.

Organs from living donors

Obviously, not all organs can be taken from a living donor, as some organs, such as the heart and lungs, are vital to the donor's own life. However, bone marrow, blood components, a lobe of the liver and a single kidney may be taken without affecting the donor's health. Doctors must be very sure that the donor understands any risks he or she may be taking – for example, a general anaesthetic may be a significant risk for some people, especially those with organs that have been weakened by disease. Doctors must also be sure that the donor is donating his or her organ willingly and is not being forced into it by other people. In some countries, such as Iran and India, people sell organs for money. However, in most countries, giving or receiving payment for organs and tissues, with the exception of blood donations, is illegal.

Organs from the patient A patient can donate his or her own tissues and fluids for transplant. One example is blood taken from a patient before an operation, stored, and then used for transfusion back into the patient during or after the operation. Another example is skin tissue taken from one part of the body and used to repair damaged skin at another part of the body. Because no material from another

CUTTING EDGE   FACTS

How can you become a donor?

It is not difficult to become an organ donor, but different countries have different regulations. In some countries, donor information is included on driving licences, while in other countries separate donor cards may be carried. In the UK, people can carry a donor card, but unless they have it with them at all times their wishes may not be followed. Registering with the NHS Organ Donor Register is a more reliable way of ensuring a person's organs will be donated. People under 16 years old can register as long as they have the consent of their parent or guardian. Older people can register as long as their organs are healthy. In the USA, regulations differ from one state to another. For example, in California, a person must be 18 or older to register fully and, although a person can join the registry between the ages of 13 and 17, a parent or guardian must make the final decision about whether or not a young person's organs can be donated.

source is used, rejection is very unlikely and the success rates of such transplants are extremely high.

Organs from related donors For a transplant to be successful, the transplanted organ or tissue must match the patient's own tissues as closely as possible. The donor and patient must have the same blood group. They must also have the same, or very similar, tissue types. Tissue type is determined by the genetic information carried in every cell in the body. This genetic information determines our body features and characteristics such as eye colour and nose shape. It also determines characteristics that we cannot see, such as blood group and tissue type. In the same way that members of a family often have similar physical characteristics, they also often have similar tissue types. Tissue types of siblings (brothers and sisters) or parents and children are usually the closest matches. Transplants between close relatives therefore often have the best chance of being successful.

Organs from unrelated donors If there is no suitable related donor, an organ from an unrelated donor may be used instead. Rigorous testing is essential to ensure that the donor has a very close tissue type match – without this, the transplant is unlikely to succeed.

CUTTING EDGE   SCIENCE

Using organs from living donors

Many factors must be taken into account when considering using an organ from a living donor. Obviously, donating the organ must not harm the donor, so the donor's general health and ability to recover from the operation are important considerations. The quality of the organ they can donate is also important as only healthy organs are suitable for transplantation. Medical staff must also be very sure that the donor is offering the organ of their own free will and is not being forced into it either by other family members or by their own sense of duty or responsibility. Medical staff must be sure that donors really understand what they are agreeing to and are fully aware of any possible health consequences. For example, kidney donors should be aware that if their remaining kidney fails, they will require a kidney transplant themselves.

Databases of tissue types of people who are willing to be donors are kept. When a patient needs a transplant, a search of the database can quickly locate a suitable donor. If none is shown on the database, a wider search, often involving databases in other countries, is carried out. If still no suitable donor is found, appeals for people to volunteer for testing may be made in the media. In some cases, unrelated donors remain anonymous, and neither patient nor donor, nor their families, know anything about each other. In other cases, patient and donor and their families do have information about each other and may even meet.

This technician is analysing samples to check their tissue types in order to ensure their suitability for organ transplants.

After removal from the donor, this kidney has been rapidly transported to the operating theatre for immediate transplant into the recipient. It is vital that organs for transplantation are kept moist, sterile and at a suitable temperature during transportation.

Organs from other transplant patients This might sound odd – how can a patient who has received a transplant have an organ to donate to somebody else? One situation where this may occur is when a patient (A) has a healthy heart but diseased lungs, and another patient (B) has healthy lungs but a diseased heart. The tissue types of patient A and patient B must match. It can be more successful to perform a combined heart and lung transplant than a lung transplant alone. This means that patient A's heart and lungs are removed and replaced with the combined heart and lungs from a person C who has died. Patient A's healthy heart can then be separated from the diseased lungs and transplanted on its own into patient B. This way, both patient A and patient B benefit from the heart and lungs of the dead person C. This type of transplant is called a 'domino transplant' because the first means the second can happen – just as knocking one domino over makes another one fall.

Organs from people who have died

Many people who die have perfectly healthy organs that could help other people live. This is often the case with people who are killed in traffic accidents. For example, a person who dies from head injuries may have a perfectly healthy heart, lungs, liver, pancreas and kidneys. These could all be used to save the lives of other people who are waiting for a transplant of one of these organs. Many people carry a donor card or have registered with an organ donor organization, giving instructions about which organs may be used after their death. Without a donor card, medical staff may ask relatives for their consent to remove organs. Making such decisions immediately after a loved one has died can be extremely difficult, and many organs that could have saved other people's lives are wasted.

CUTTING EDGE MOMENTS

Domino transplants

Domino transplants occur quite rarely. The first was carried out in 1987 in Baltimore, Maryland, USA. Clinton House's lungs were incurably damaged by cystic fibrosis, an inherited lung disease. Surgeons thought that a combined heart-lung transplant would be more successful than a lung transplant alone. Clinton House received the heart and lungs from a traffic accident victim. Clinton's own healthy heart was transplanted into another man, John Couch, who suffered from untreatable heart failure. In this way, the heart and lungs from a single person saved the lives of two people.

Sometimes organs are removed from people who are not technically dead, but are not really alive either, in the usual sense of the word. With modern technology it is possible to keep a person 'alive' long after they would, in the absence of such technology, have died. Doctors have to be absolutely certain that there is no possibility of such a person recovering before they remove any organs for transplant.

There are strict guidelines about this. In most countries, tests on the person must be carried out by two independent doctors, neither of whom is involved in a transplant programme, at least 24 hours apart. Using an electroencephalogram (EEG), doctors can monitor electrical activity in the brain. If there is no electrical activity in the brain, the person is considered to be 'brain dead'. This means that the brain is so badly damaged that it cannot carry out any functions at all, not even basic life processes such as maintaining breathing. There is no chance of recovery and so, at that stage, organs may be removed for transplantation. If there is any electrical activity, the patient may have some chance of recovery and, however limited that recovery may be, the patient's continued existence must take priority over any potential transplants.

Living donors can donate organs and tissues such as bone marrow, blood, skin, a single kidney and parts of their liver, lung, small intestine and pancreas. From a deceased donor, though, vital organs such as heart and lungs can also be removed and used for transplants to benefit many people. For example, using corneas, kidneys, heart, lungs, liver, small intestine and pancreas from a

CUTTING EDGE   DEBATES

Attitudes to transplants

Many people think that organ transplants are good because they help to save lives. Other people disapprove of transplants for cultural or religious reasons. Some believe that scientists should be allowed to make as much progress as possible in the field of organ transplantation. Others believe that, by carrying out transplants, humans are meddling in things that they should leave to God or some other higher power. Some believe that it is wrong to mix parts of different people together while others think that this does not matter. It is all a matter of opinion. What do you think?

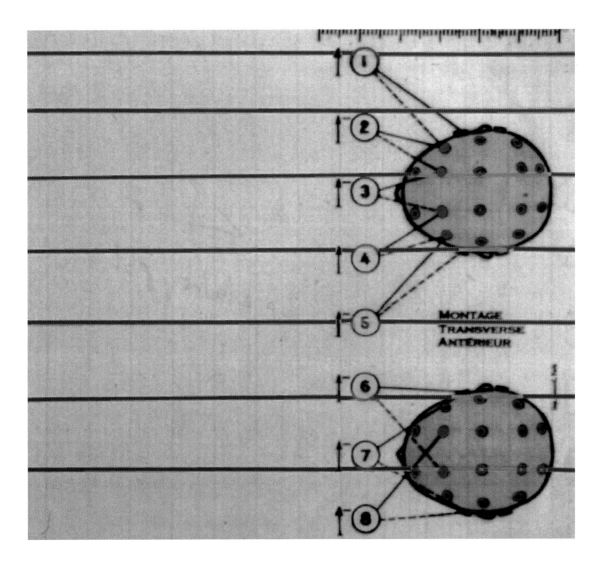

single donor could benefit as many as eleven different people – and even more may benefit if tissues such as bone, skin and bone marrow are used as well.

Organs from other sources Because there are always more people waiting for transplants than there are organs available, scientists have searched for other sources of organs. Organs from animals such as cows and pigs have been used. Artificial organs, such as mechanical hearts, have been developed. Stem cells, which are cells that can develop into any type of cell, may in the future be used to grow new organs in the laboratory. Each of these is discussed in more detail in Chapters 5 and 6.

The flat brainwaves in this EEG show that there are no electrical impulses being produced by the brain. The brain is regarded as dead. To obtain an EEG, electrodes are attached to a person's head – their locations are shown as pink dots on the heads on the right.

The Transplantation Process

Every transplant operation requires careful planning and organization. A suitable organ must be found and transported to the correct place within very tight time limits. At the same time, the patient must be assessed and prepared for the operation. The operation requires skilled surgical and other medical staff. After the operation, the patient must be monitored carefully. It requires a large team of people to ensure that the whole transplantation process is carried out smoothly and efficiently.

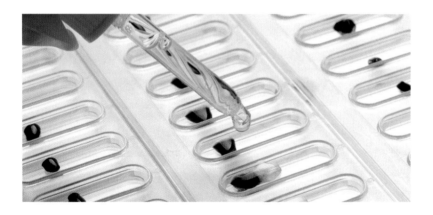

Here, a patient's blood group is being checked. A pipette is used to add blood group B antibodies to some samples of blood. The antibodies will react with any B antigens on the red blood cells in the samples, making the cells agglutinate, or clump together.

The first step in the transplantation process is the assessment of a patient, to see whether he or she could benefit from a transplant. This involves rigorous physical and psychological testing. The patient's condition must be serious enough to require a transplant, yet the patient must be well enough in other ways to stand up to the surgery involved. Doctors also need to be sure that the patient would be able to cope mentally with the transplant and to take regularly all the medicines that would be necessary after the operation. The patient also needs to be able to cope with the dampening of the immune system caused by the immunosuppressive drugs, so he or she cannot suffer from a condition that would be made worse by this. For example, the patient cannot suffer from active untreated cancer or have AIDS.

Once a patient has been identified as needing and being suitable for a transplant, the search for a suitable organ begins. National and international registers keep up-to-date information about available donors and organs. The patient's tissue type is checked from a blood sample. The blood cells are separated and mixed with specific antibodies (chemicals produced by the immune system when it meets something foreign.) Each antibody matches one antigen (a foreign protein that stimulates antibody production.) If an antigen that matches the antibody is present on the blood cells, the antibody sticks to it. Laboratory instruments detect when an antibody and antigen have stuck together. By putting together all the results, scientists can work out which antigens are present in the blood sample. From that information they can work out the person's tissue type, which is vital when matching patient and organ. It may be a long wait, but once a match between an organ and the patient has been found, preparations for the operation can begin.

CUTTING EDGE   SCIENCE

Waiting for transplants
The length of time a person has to wait for a transplant depends on several factors including:

- blood group and tissue type – people with rare blood groups and tissue types often have to wait longer for a match than people with more common combinations;
- the type of organ needed – some organs (such as kidneys and corneas) are more readily available than others;
- medical urgency – if only a single organ is available, the patient with the greatest medical need will receive it while others wait;
- time already spent on waiting list – a person who has already waited a long time for an organ may receive one in preference to a person who has waited for a shorter time;
- distance – the shorter the travelling distance between the organ and the patient, the more successful the transplant is likely to be.

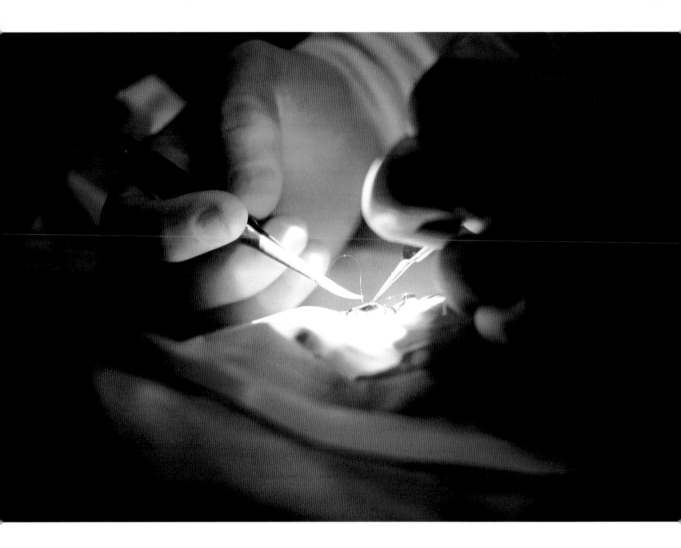

As soon as the patient has been notified that an organ is available, he or she needs to get to the hospital quickly. At the same time the organ will begin its journey to the hospital. Before the transplant can go ahead, the patient's health must be assessed again. The transplant may be cancelled if the patient has an infection or if there is any other problem.

A surgeon stitches a donated cornea onto a recipient's eye during a corneal transplant operation.

Corneal transplants

Corneal transplants may be needed if a patient's own cornea (the clear layer covering the front of the eye) is damaged through injury or illness. The cornea is first removed from a deceased donor. The transplant operation, which is also known as keratoplasty, is usually carried out with a local anaesthetic. This means that the patient is awake throughout the surgery but feels no pain because the eye is numb. The operation is carried out using a surgical microscope, an instrument that gives the surgeon a magnified view of the eye as he or she operates. The eye is measured and the donor cornea is cut to the right size and shape. An instrument called a trephine is used to cut out the damaged part of the patient's cornea. The donor cornea is then positioned carefully and stitched into place. After the operation the eye is protected with a soft patch and a hard shield to prevent any damage. Eye drops are administered regularly to minimize any risk of rejection. The stitches may be removed after a few months or may be left in place permanently. Vision usually returns slowly, with most patients regaining good eyesight within a year. Because the cornea has virtually no blood supply, rejection of the transplant is unlikely.

CUTTING EDGE — SCIENCE

How are organs kept 'alive' outside the body?

After removal from a donor, an organ for transplant must be kept in the best possible condition to ensure it does not deteriorate and to give the transplant the best chance of succeeding. To achieve this, the organ is chilled and kept in sterile saline solution (a solution containing salt and water, which acts as a temporary substitute for blood). The transplant must be carried out as soon as possible after removal. For example, kidneys must be used within 48 hours of removal, livers within 8 to 20 hours, hearts and lungs within 5 to 6 hours, and corneas within 4 weeks. Organs from living donors are usually removed at the same hospital where the transplant will be carried out. Organs from dead donors are taken to the transplant hospital by the fastest means of transport.

Bone marrow transplants

Some forms of anaemia, leukaemia, Hodgkin's Disease and other white blood cell cancers and tumours damage bone marrow. This prevents normal production of white blood cells and so the immune system cannot function properly. Bone marrow transplants can restore white blood cell production and immune function.

Before a bone marrow transplant is carried out, the patient usually receives very high doses of radiotherapy (radiation treatment) and chemotherapy (drug treatment). These treatments destroy the patient's immune system so that it cannot attack the transplanted cells. It also kills any diseased cells such as cancer cells. The bone marrow cells are then transplanted into the patient by 'infusion'. This means that they are delivered directly into the patient's bloodstream through a tube inserted into a vein, called an intravenous (IV) tube.

Once in the bloodstream, the transplanted cells move to the patient's bone marrow, where they grow and produce new blood cells. The number of the blood cells in the patient's blood is monitored for several weeks until doctors are sure the transplant has worked and new blood cells are being produced. During this time, the patient needs to be protected from infection.

CUTTING EDGE   FACTS

How long do transplant operations take?

There are no absolute figures for how long a transplant operation takes. There are differences between every organ and between every patient, so every operation is different, too. This table gives some average operation times, but individual operations can be significantly longer or shorter than these.

Organ to be transplanted	Average length of transplant operation
cornea	less than 1 hour
bone marrow	1–5 hours
kidney	2–4 hours
heart	3–4 hours
liver	5–6 hours

Kidney and pancreas transplants

Kidneys filter waste chemicals and excess water from the blood. If the kidneys do not work properly, the blood does not get 'cleaned' and the person can become extremely ill. Kidney failure can be caused by several conditions, including diabetes, hypertension (very high blood pressure) and glomerulonephritis (chronic kidney inflammation).

A kidney transplant is carried out while the patient is under a general anaesthetic. First, the kidney is removed from the donor. If the donor is living, he or she is given a general anaesthetic. Microsurgical methods (surgery carried out through several small incisions and using magnified views and special instruments) are often used to minimize the surgery necessary for the donor. It is important that a small part of each of the kidney's main blood vessels, the renal artery and renal vein, are left attached to the kidney. A small length of the ureter, the tube that carries urine from the kidney to the bladder, must also be left attached to the kidney. An incision is then made in the patient's abdomen, above the pelvic bones, and the kidney is carefully put into place. The renal artery and renal vein are stitched to the major blood vessels that carry blood to and from the leg. The ureter is stitched to the patient's bladder, and finally the incision made in the abdomen is stitched. The amount of fluid drunk and urine produced will be monitored closely to ensure the transplanted kidney begins to function.

The kidney shown here has been removed from the donor and is being prepared for transplant. The surgeon is removing fat from the kidney. The blood vessels of the organ must also be flushed through with a special solution before it is ready to be transplanted.

A pancreas transplant is carried out in a similar way to a kidney transplant. The patient's own pancreas is not removed, and the new pancreas is transplanted into the lower abdomen. Again, the blood vessels of the pancreas are attached to the blood vessels of the leg. As well as secreting insulin into the blood, the pancreas also secretes other substances via a duct (tube) into part of the small intestine. Therefore a small piece of donor small intestine, with the duct draining into it, is removed at the same time. The donor intestine is surgically attached to the recipient's bladder or intestine to drain the secretions from the donor pancreas after the operation.

Some patients who are diabetic (see page 15) also suffer kidney failure, and a pancreas transplant alone would not solve their problems. In such cases, a kidney and pancreas can be transplanted at the same time. As with the single organ transplants, the patient's own kidneys and pancreas are left in place and the new organs transplanted into the lower abdomen.

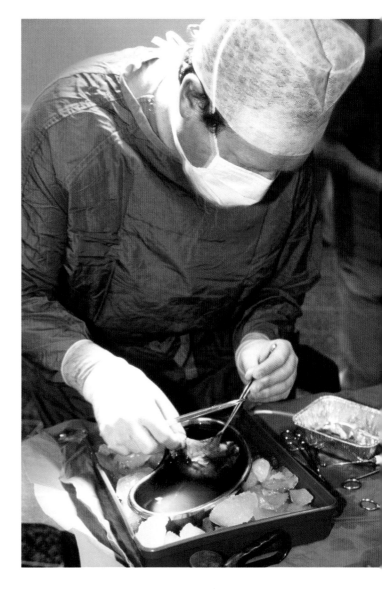

Heart transplants

A heart transplant may be necessary in a patient whose own heart is failing or has failed. A major cause of heart failure is coronary heart disease (often caused by smoking, lack of exercise, obesity or eating too many fatty foods). Another major cause of heart failure is cardiomyopathy, in which the heart muscle fails. Heart failure can also have genetic origins.

Patients waiting for a heart transplant are usually extremely ill and often close to death. Symptoms of acute heart failure include weakness, pallor and shortness of breath. Many are confined to a wheelchair or their bed and may at best be able to walk a few steps. They often need an oxygen supply to help them to breathe. For patients like this, a heart transplant is not just a lifesaving operation, it also allows them to lead an active life and do things they may not have been well enough to do for years.

A heart transplant is carried out while the patient is under a general anaesthetic. An incision is made through the sternum, and the chest is opened. The patient's blood supply is connected to a heart-lung machine that will take over the function of the heart and

CUTTING EDGE SCIENTISTS

Sir Magdi Yacoub

Heart transplant surgeon Magdi Yacoub was born in a village in Egypt on 16 November 1935. His father was a general surgeon and Magdi knew when he was a young boy that he wanted to be a surgeon, too. Magdi was educated in Cairo and qualified as a doctor there in 1957. In 1962, he moved to London, where he became a consultant cardiac surgeon. Magdi specialized in working with children with congenital heart defects (defects they were born with) and carried out many complex operations on very young babies. He was also involved with the first heart transplant in the UK and performed the first live lobe lung transplant (using a lobe of lung from a living donor) in the UK.

Magdi Yacoub retired in 2001 but is still involved in research into organ rejection, development of artificial heart valves, stem cells and xenotransplantation (transplantation of animal organs into humans). He has received many awards for his outstanding work and was knighted in 1992. Magdi has always tried to help others and he set up the Chain of Hope charity to provide free heart treatment to sick children from poor and war-torn countries.

Sir Magdi Yacoub is famous for his pioneering work in heart transplant surgery.

lungs during the operation in order to keep the patient alive. The diseased heart is removed and the new heart put into the chest cavity and stitched into place. The blood vessels are reconnected and blood flows through the transplanted heart. This may begin to beat on its own, but if it does not, surgeons may trigger it with an electric shock. Once a regular heartbeat is established, the patient is disconnected from the heart-lung machine. The chest cavity is closed with stitches or clips. These are removed about one week after surgery. The patient will need to spend some time under close supervision in intensive care, but should be able to get up within a few days.

Lung transplants

In the lungs, waste carbon dioxide is removed from the blood and oxygen enters the blood. If the lungs are damaged so that this cannot occur, a lung transplant may be necessary.

With the patient under a general anaesthetic, a large incision is made in the chest. For a single lung transplant, this may be either through the sternum or horizontally from below the shoulder blade around the side to the front. The surgeon collapses the diseased lung and severs the blood vessels and airway. The lung can then be removed, the new lung put in its place and the airway and blood vessels reconnected. Throughout the operation the remaining lung continues to function normally. For a double lung transplant, the incision is under the ribcage, from one armpit to the other. The single lung transplant process is then carried out twice over. At some point during this operation, the patient will probably need to be connected to a heart-lung machine.

Once the lung or lungs have been stitched into place, the chest incision is closed and stitched or clipped. The air that remains in

In this liver transplant operation, the donated liver is ready to be stitched into place in the recipient's abdomen. The ice helps to keep the liver fresh.

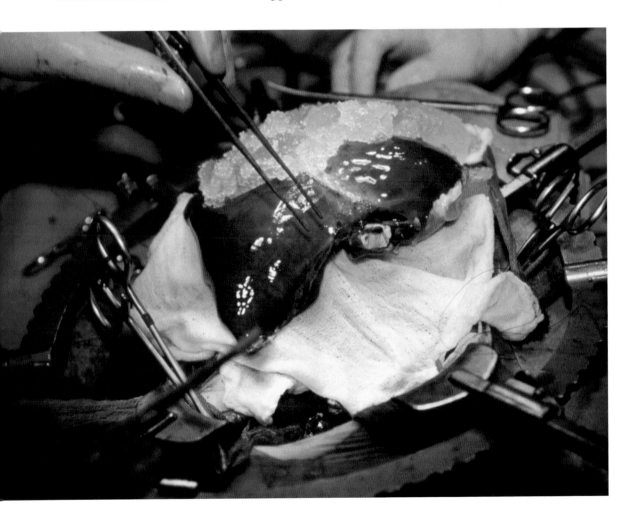

CUTTING EDGE — SCIENCE

Variations on basic transplants

In some cases, variations on a basic heart, lung or liver transplant are required. These include:

- In some patients, the heart and both lungs are damaged. These patients may receive a combined heart and lung transplant using similar techniques to those described above.
- A split liver transplant can also be carried out. In this operation, a liver is split into two, with part of it going to one patient and part of it going to another. This is possible because a person can be healthy with less than a whole liver. Because of the liver's structure, it cannot be split exactly in half, so the patient with the greater need receives the larger portion (60 per cent) and the other patient receives the smaller (40 per cent). In this way, two patients can have lifesaving treatment from a single liver.

the chest cavity from the operation is removed via a drain to allow the transplanted lung to reinflate. This drain is removed when the chest wound heals. After the operation, the patient will need to spend several days in intensive care and may need the assistance of a mechanical ventilator to carry out the normal functions of the lungs until the patient's own lungs are fully functioning again.

Liver transplants

Liver failure may make a liver transplant necessary. Two major causes of liver failure are alcohol abuse and infection by the disease Hepatitis C. Another cause of liver failure is primary biliary cirrhosis, a condition in which liver tissue is slowly destroyed.

With the patient under a general anaesthetic, a large, curved incision is made in the upper part of the abdomen. The patient's liver is removed and the new liver is put in its place. Blood vessels and bile ducts are reattached. A small tube may be put in to drain fluid away from the bile duct. This fluid is collected in a small bag outside the body. Other tubes may also be inserted to drain fluid from around the liver. The liver is stitched into place and the abdominal incision is closed and stitched. A short period of close monitoring in intensive care will be needed. When the patient has recovered and is ready to leave hospital, the drains are removed.

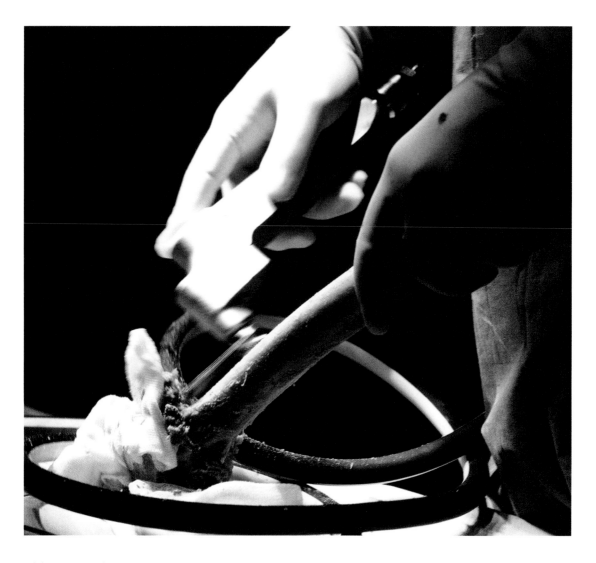

Skin transplants

If skin is so badly damaged that it cannot repair itself, a skin transplant may be needed. Skin transplants are often necessary in cases of severe burns, large wounds, some surgical procedures and some cosmetic surgery.

Depending on how extensive the skin damage is, a skin transplant may be carried out under local or general anaesthetic. To use a patient's own skin for repairing a small area, a skin-cutting instrument called a dermatome is used to remove skin from another part of the body such as the buttock or inner thigh. The graft is spread over the damaged area and is held in place by a padded dressing or stitches. The area from where the graft is taken must

A surgeon prepares donated bone for a bone transplant operation. The surgeon is using a tool to shape the bone before it is implanted.

CUTTING EDGE   FACTS

How do patients feel after a transplant?

How a patient feels after a transplant differs depending on the type of organ that has been transplanted. For example, you would expect a patient who has received a corneal transplant to feel very different from one who has received a heart transplant. Once the initial recovery period after surgery is over, most transplant patients feel much better than they did before the transplant. Their quality of life is much improved and they are able to do many things that their ill-health previously prevented. Most transplant recipients are extremely grateful to the donor who made the operation possible. Occasionally, a patient is unable to accept the fact that his or her body contains part of somebody else, and the patient may suffer psychological problems.

also be covered with a dressing to prevent infection. For a larger area of damage, a flap of skin together with underlying muscle and blood supply may be transplanted. The transplant will need to be monitored for several weeks to ensure a blood circulation is established, and patients are often advised to avoid stretching the transplanted area during this time.

Bone tissue transplants

Bone tissue transplants are carried out for several reasons, including reconstruction of damaged or deformed bones and bone repair after treatment for bone cancer.

A bone tissue transplant can be used to replace or repair damaged bone. The operation is usually carried out under a general anaesthetic. An incision is made in the skin above the bone. The bone tissue that is to be transplanted is shaped to fit and then inserted into the space where it is needed. It is held in place with screws, pins or plates. The incision is then closed and stitched. To prevent the transplanted bone tissue from moving while it is healing, a splint or plaster cast is often used. The length of the recovery period varies, depending on how much bone tissue was transplanted and the site of the transplant. A patient is often advised to limit the amount of exercise he or she undertakes for several months after the transplant in order to allow the bone to heal fully.

After the operation

A patient's health continues to be monitored for a long time after a transplant operation. Initially, while the patient is still in hospital, his or her condition will be monitored almost continuously. Some tests and checks are specific to a particular type of transplant. For example, most lung transplant patients undergo lung function tests, such as exercising while being monitored with a spirometer. The condition of the lungs themselves are checked by bronchoscopy, chest X-ray and CT scan. Heart function in most heart transplant patients is checked by electrocardiogram (ECG) and echocardiogram, and the condition of the heart may be checked by chest X-ray and CT scan.

There are also general tests that are carried out following most types of transplant. These include:

- blood tests – the levels of a variety of chemicals in the blood provide information about how well the transplanted organ and other organs are functioning.
- blood count – checking the number of red blood cells, white blood cells and platelets provides information about the health of the patient.
- biopsy – examining a tiny sample of the transplanted organ allows medical staff to check for early signs of rejection.

The number and frequency of tests will gradually be reduced as the patient's recovery progresses, but the patient may still need to

CUTTING EDGE SCIENCE

How do immunosuppressive drugs work?

Different immunosuppressive drugs work in different ways, but they all affect the white blood cells to stop them from attacking the transplant. Some block the production and development of new white blood cells. Some, such as cortisone, prevent white blood cells from causing inflammation of the tissue of the organ that is being rejected. Others, such as cyclosporine, prevent white blood cells from producing interleukin-2, a hormone that is needed for the immune system to mount an effective immune response.

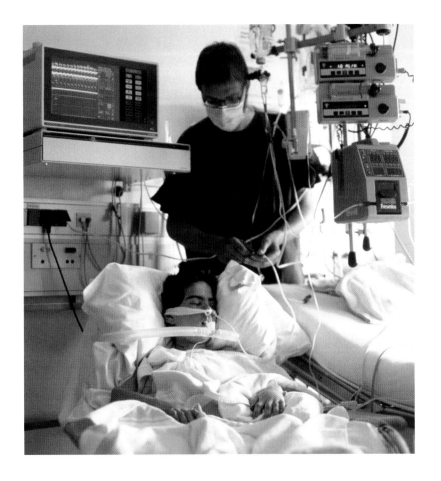

This patient is recovering in a cardiac intensive care unit (ICU). The monitor shows information such as his heart rate and breathing rate.

attend clinics for check-ups several times a week for a while. If all goes well, the patient stays healthy and the transplant is not rejected, the time between one check-up and the next will gradually be increased. Many transplant patients have a yearly check-up for the rest of their lives.

Immunosuppression

The main danger after a transplant is rejection – even when tissue types have been carefully matched, the patient's body may reject the transplanted organ. To prevent this from happening the patient must take a combination of drugs to stop his or her immune system from working. This is called immunosuppression. However, the drugs do not just stop the immune system from attacking the transplant, they stop it from attacking anything at all. The patient is therefore unable to resist infections and may need strong antibiotics to combat this risk.

CHAPTER 5

Overcoming Problems in Organ Transplantation

O rgan transplantation may seem like a miracle treatment for some illnesses and conditions that would otherwise be fatal. However, although it can save lives, it does also raise some problems.

Organ shortage

One of the biggest problems surrounding organ transplantation is the shortage of organs. National and international transplant programmes hold information about donors and about patients who are waiting for transplants. They act rapidly to match donors and patients to ensure that no organ is wasted. International co-operation allows donors and patients from around the world to be matched.

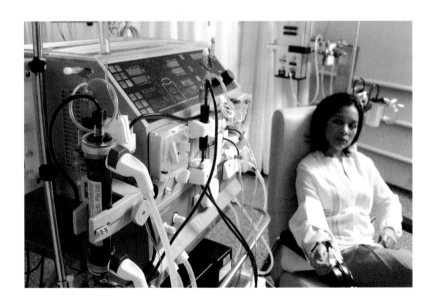

Many patients with kidney failure depend on dialysis machines like this one. The process of filtering the blood takes several hours.

Another way of tackling the problem of the shortage of organs is to find something else that can be used to replace a failing organ. At present, no organ substitute is ideal for long-term use and most are used simply to keep a patient alive while he or she waits for an organ transplant. Developing artificial organs has been more successful for some organs than others.

Artificial organs

Dialysis machines have been generally available since the 1960s as a mechanical substitute for the blood-filtering function of the kidneys. A tube carries blood from the patient's arm into the dialysis machine, which removes waste chemicals and ensures the correct levels of minerals, salts, sugar and water are maintained. The blood then flows back into the patient's arm via a second tube. For many patients, dialysis means lengthy hospital visits several times a week, which can disrupt a child's education and make it impossible for an adult to stay in employment.

Smaller devices have been developed for patients to use in their own homes, but these take up considerable space. They are also costly, and so are not available for every patient who would benefit from them. A more recent innovation is a portable device, coupled with an osmotic membrane (a thin layer that allows some substances to pass through it) implanted into the abdomen. The device must be connected to a small external machine, usually on a daily basis, to complete the dialysis process.

CUTTING EDGE **FACTS**

Finding more donors
In some countries, people who wish to become donors have to register with the appropriate organization. Because of all the information checking that this system entails, vital time can be lost between a person dying and the organs being released for transplant. Some governments are considering turning the system the other way around so that everybody would be assumed to be a willing donor unless they had registered their refusal. However, although this would increase the number of organs available for transplantation, some people oppose the idea and the matter is still under discussion. Advertising and education are also being used to make more people aware of the organ shortage and to persuade them to register as organ donors.

However, none of these methods of dialysis provides an ideal long-term solution, and the majority of patients with kidney failure look forward to having a transplant that will allow them to resume a more normal life.

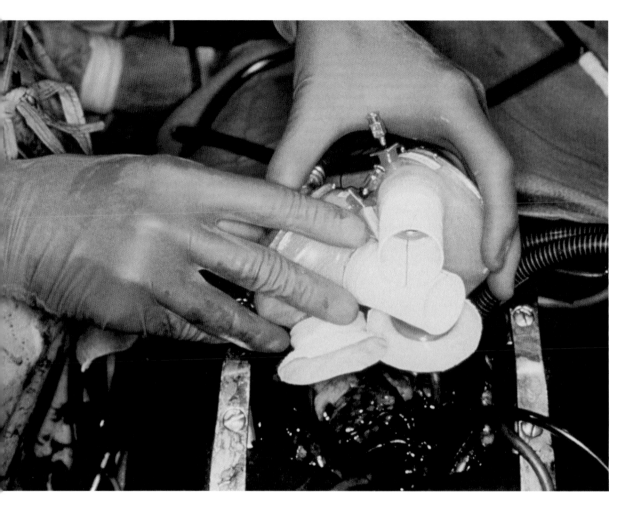

The development of an artificial heart has long been a goal for many scientists. The first was patented in 1963 in Utah, USA, by Paul Winchell. His design formed the starting point for Robert Jarvik, working at the University of Utah, USA, who developed an artificial heart called the Jarvik-7. This was first used at the University of Utah Medical Center, Salt Lake City, Utah, USA, on a 61-year-old retired dentist, Barney Clark, on 2 December 1982. He survived for 112 days after the operation, which encouraged scientists to continue working on this design. However, the Jarvik-7 and other subsequent models all required external power supplies such as large battery packs. The battery packs were heavy and about the size of a refrigerator, restricting the patient's mobility.

On 2 July 2001, a 59-year-old retired librarian, Robert Tools, received the first AbioCor Implantable Replacement Heart at a hospital

A Jarvik-7 artificial heart is implanted into a patient's chest.

in Louisville, Kentucky, USA. It was made of special plastic and titanium, making it safe for contact with blood, and it had few moving parts. What was revolutionary about the AbioCor was the fact that, as well as an external battery pack, it had internal batteries that could power it for up to half an hour. This allowed patients to disconnect themselves from the external battery pack for short periods, for example while they took a shower or bath.

Another milestone in the development of an artificial heart was the introduction of the Berlin Heart. This sits outside the body and should more properly be called a ventricular assist device (VAD). It can help either of the ventricles of the heart to pump blood. The ventricles are the lower chambers of the heart that receive blood from the upper chambers and pump it to the arteries. If both ventricles are failing, two Berlin Hearts can be used, one for each ventricle. The pump, which is driven by compressed air, stays outside the body and is connected to the heart and blood vessels by tubes. Although they have been used in isolated cases in the USA, Berlin Hearts have not been approved for general use there. Other types of VAD can be used, though, and some can be fitted inside the chest, 'piggybacking' the patient's own heart.

CUTTING EDGE MOMENTS

Artificial hearts for babies and children

Some babies are born with defective hearts, and others develop heart problems during childhood. Many of these babies and children can be treated by surgery. However, in some cases, a heart transplant is the only option. If a child becomes dangerously ill while waiting for a donor heart, the child may receive an artificial heart to get through the waiting period. This has only become possible in recent years as the small size of a baby's or young child's body has made it difficult to develop a suitable artificial device. An ECMO (extra-corporeal membrane oxygenator) machine can take over the function of the heart and lungs for up to 21 days, after which complications such as blood clots, internal bleeding or kidney problems often develop. With the development of the Berlin Heart, which can be made as small as a golf ball, even very young babies can be helped. Since the first one was used in 1990, Berlin Hearts have saved many children's lives during the wait for a transplant.

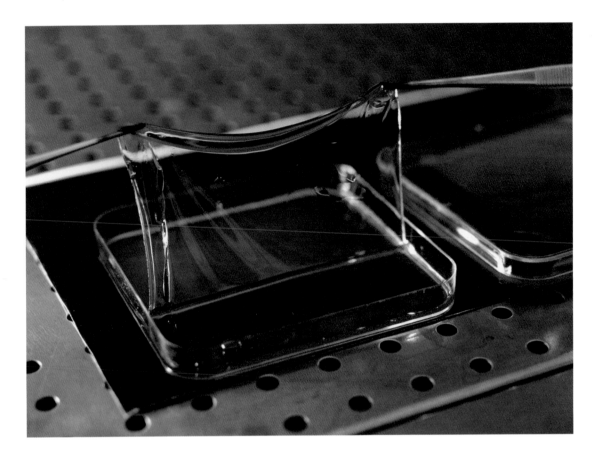

Patients waiting for a liver transplant may receive an artificial liver. This combines a pump and cloned (grown from a single cell in the laboratory) human liver cells. As blood is pumped through the device, the liver cells carry out normal liver functions such as filtering out toxins and producing proteins and other chemicals.

For patients waiting for a lung transplant, implantable synthetic lungs (intravenous membrane oxygenators, or IMOs) can be used as a temporary measure. An IMO is a bundle of hollow fibres with a balloon at the centre. It is injected into a vein in the leg and guided through the blood vessels to the vena cava, the large blood vessel that carries blood to the heart. Once in position, the balloon inflates and deflates about a hundred times a minute, drawing blood through the fibres. Oxygen enters the blood and waste carbon dioxide is removed.

Artificial skin has been developed and transplanted successfully by a number of research teams, including one at the University of Illinois, Chicago, USA. One method combines natural collagen, a

Artificially grown skin is removed from a culture dish ready for use in a skin transplant operation. It takes just three weeks to grow a square metre of skin. The artificial skin can be used to help burns victims whose injuries are so severe there is little healthy skin left from which to make a skin graft.

fibrous material, and a synthetic polymer mesh (human-made netting). Micro-sponges of collagen are formed in the spaces of the polymer mesh. This provides a framework on which skin cells can grow. The resulting substance, when used to cover an area of damaged skin, supports the growth and development of new skin. An alternative substance is a self-repairing artificial skin. This contains microcapsules that are filled with a healing chemical. If the artificial skin cracks, the microcapsules break open and the chemical is released into the crack, helping to repair it.

Growing new organs

Another approach to overcoming the shortage of organs is to find a way of growing new ones. Some teams of scientists are hoping that stem cells (see panel) may offer a way of doing this. By taking stem cells and growing them in the laboratory, they hope to be able to use a patient's own stem cells to grow new tissues and organs for transplant.

It may also be possible to use other body cells for growing new organs. In April 2006, doctors in the USA reported that they had successfully grown new bladders from patients' own bladder cells and then transplanted them back into the patients. The advantage of using a patient's own cells is that the organs are the same blood and tissue type as the patient's, so there is no risk of rejection.

Rejection of transplants

A second major problem with organ transplantation is the rejection of a transplant by the patient's immune system. There are two main ways of trying to combat this. One is to ensure that the organ and

CUTTING EDGE SCIENCE

What are stem cells?

Every cell in the human body contains a full set of genetic information. At the earliest stage of a cell's development it has the potential to become any type of cell and is called a stem cell. The stem cell's genetic information instructs it to develop in a particular way so that it matures into a specific type of cell, such as a skin cell or muscle cell. It cannot then change into any other type of cell.

the patient are as similar as possible. This is achieved by accurate tissue typing, which enables close matching of the organ and the patient. The smaller the differences between the tissue types of the organ and the patient, the less likelihood there is of the patient's immune system recognizing the organ as foreign and attacking it. The other way of avoiding rejection is to suppress (restrain) the patient's immune system. To do this, radiotherapy (treatment involving radiation), immunosuppressive drugs, or a combination of both, are used. If the immune system is suppressed, it cannot attack the organ and so rejection does not occur.

Early attempts at immunosuppression used radiotherapy alone. Then, during the 1960s, a limited number of immunosuppressive drugs became available. For more than twenty years, combinations of these were used. More sophisticated approaches were developed during the 1970s with the introduction of drugs that target specific cells in the immune system. As scientists expand their knowledge and understanding of the mechanics of the immune system, they may be able to develop drugs that work in a more targeted way and so have fewer harmful effects on the rest of the body.

CUTTING EDGE   SCIENCE

What are the risks with immunosuppression?

Although immunosuppression helps to prevent rejection, it also causes some problems. One function of the body's immune system is to provide protection against germs. Suppressing a patient's immune system therefore makes a patient vulnerable to infections caused by germs. An infection that may pose little risk to a relatively healthy person, such as a common cold, can quickly get out of control and be life-threatening for someone with a suppressed immune system.

Another function of the immune system is to detect and destroy abnormal cells such as cancer cells. A suppressed immune system cannot do this, so immunosuppression leads to an increased risk of cancer. Radiotherapy and immunosuppressive drugs themselves can also have unpleasant side effects such as hair loss, vomiting, diarrhoea, kidney and liver damage and digestive system problems. Radiotherapy has this effect because it targets not only cancer cells but all swiftly dividing cells in the body, including the hair follicles and intestinal lining. The destruction of these cells causes the above-mentioned side effects.

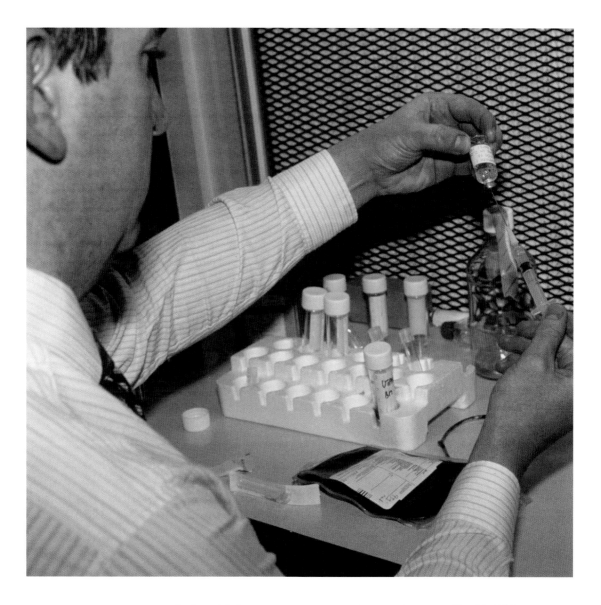

In some cases, particularly with bone marrow transplants, the opposite to rejection can happen: the immune system cells in the transplanted organ can react to the patient's own cells. This is called a graft-versus-host (GVH) reaction. If it arises, it is treated with high doses of powerful drugs.

The risk with bone marrow transplants is that the transplant will reject the recipient. To help avoid this possibility, this doctor is adding special antibodies to the donor bone marrow in order to purge it of the white blood cells that might launch the attack.

Surgical techniques

Carrying out an organ transplant operation requires a high level of surgical skill. There has been considerable progress in surgical techniques since the earliest transplant operations were carried out.

Consequently, transplant procedures carry less risk than they did some years ago.

Progress in surgical techniques has benefited living donors as well as transplant recipients. For example, until the mid-1990s, people who donated a kidney underwent a major operation. This involved a large incision, often 25 cm long, cutting through abdominal muscle, and the removal of a rib. Today, surgeons use keyhole, or laparoscopic, surgery in which a small incision (about 7–8 cm wide) is made near the navel. Four small holes are also made in the abdomen for insertion of surgical instruments. The donor is left with a much smaller scar and is able to recover more quickly than from traditional surgery. In addition to the benefit to the donor, keyhole surgery has also increased the number of live donors, as more people are willing to undergo this less daunting procedure.

Some surgical advances have followed from developments in medical technology and equipment. For example, magnetic resonance imaging (MRI) and computed tomography (CT) scans – techniques for viewing the inside of the body – provide medical staff with valuable information both before and after surgery. Also, developments in image capture and computer technology have made it possible for detailed images to be displayed on computer

CUTTING EDGE   SCIENCE

Robot surgeons?

Robotic technology has advanced rapidly in recent years and some of these advances are proving to be of great value to surgeons. It is now possible for a surgeon to operate while sitting beside the patient and looking at a computer screen. The screen shows a detailed image of the part of the patient's body that is to undergo surgery. Special grips are connected to the computer which in turn is connected to surgical instruments that have been placed inside the patient's body. While watching the image, the surgeon moves the grips, which makes the computer move the instruments inside the patient. This amazing technology allows the surgeon to make very accurate movements, reducing patient pain following surgery (as they have a much smaller wound), and allowing a quicker recovery than normal surgery.

screens during surgery. Tiny cameras can be positioned to allow the surgeon to see organs, blood vessels and other structures from angles that would otherwise be impossible. Special lenses, worn like a pair of spectacles, create a very clear, magnified view for carrying out intricate surgery.

This patient is undergoing surgery carried out by a robot. The robotic surgical instruments are controlled by the surgeon seated on the left.

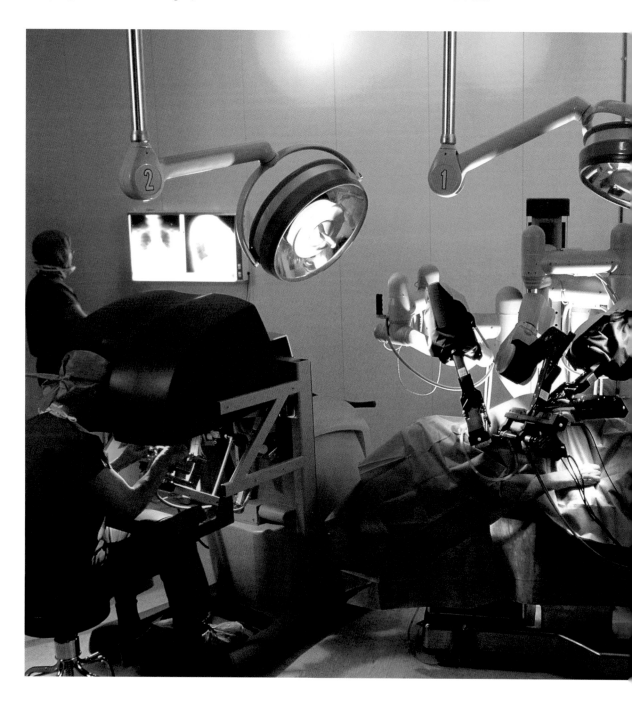

CHAPTER 6

Current Research

O ver the last fifty years, scientists and doctors working in the field of organ transplantation have made tremendous progress. However, there are still problems to be solved and the search for better technologies, deeper understanding and improved methods continues.

Stem cells

Many scientists think that stem cell research will provide significant advances in organ transplantation. Stem cells have the potential to

CUTTING EDGE   DEBATES

Ethical issues

There are many ethical issues surrounding the field of organ transplantation. Doctors, scientists, politicians, religious leaders and many other groups of people are involved in discussions about what should and should not be allowed. Different countries have different laws, and some allow procedures that are banned elsewhere. Some of the issues being debated include the following:

Is it right to:
● use animals as a source of organs, tissues, cells or fluids for humans?
● use human embryos as a source of stem cells?
● alter the genetic information in cells?
● create transgenic animals (see page 57)?

What do you think? Is any action justified if it can save a person's life, or should there be limits to what scientists are allowed to do? And if there should be limits, who should decide on those limits? And should these decisions be reviewed as science progresses?

mature and develop into every type of cell in the body. Around the world, teams of scientists are experimenting with stem cells in attempts to grow new tissues and organs. If a patient's own stem cells could be removed and stimulated to develop into a new organ, this could be used to replace a failing or diseased organ. Two of the main problems with transplants from other individuals would thus be removed. Firstly, the patient's immune system would not reject the body's own tissue, so immunosuppression would not be necessary. Secondly, there would be no shortage of organs for transplant.

Artificial organs

Scientists are also carrying out research into the development of more and better artificial organs. Early artificial organs were designed to copy the exact functioning of the human organ they were replacing. Now, many scientists believe that human organs

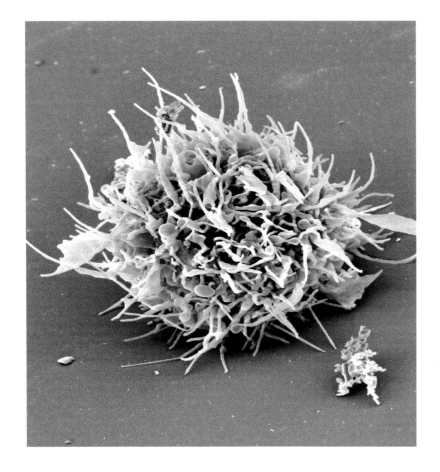

A micrograph of a human stem cell. This type of stem cell has the potential to develop into either a red or white blood cell.

are too complex for this 'mechanical copying' to be successful. Instead, they have turned their attention to growing and manipulating human cells as a means of creating organs. Attempts are also being made to develop hybrid devices, combining artificial parts with living cells. An example of this is the artificial liver (see page 48). If this is also successful for other organs, this research will provide devices that can be used instead of human organs and provide a solution to the problem of organ shortages.

CUTTING EDGE   FACTS

Hiding transplanted cells

Scientists searching for ways to combat rejection have developed materials that can be used as a barrier between transplanted cells and the recipient's body. For example, using a semipermeable polymer membrane developed at Charles University, Prague, in the Czech Republic, scientists have been able to implant cells into the brains of patients suffering from Parkinson's disease. The polymer acts as a sheath, separating the transplanted cells from the patient's cells. Once transplanted, the cells produce dopamine, a chemical necessary for normal brain function, that diffuses out through the sheath into the brain. This has led to an improvement in the condition of some patients. Doctors are hoping that a similar technique may be used to treat other illnesses such as Alzheimer's disease and diabetes. Research into the development of an ideal material for the sheath is continuing in many countries, including the USA.

Xenotransplantation

Xenotransplantation is the transplantation of organs from an animal of one species into an animal of a different species. This is another interesting field of research. However, whole organ transplants from animals that are closely related to humans, such as baboons and chimpanzees, have not been successful. The species that seems to be most promising for transplantation of organs into humans is the pig, as the organs are similar in size to human organs. Pig organs are also in plentiful supply as litter sizes are large, pigs are easy to rear and they grow quickly. Since 1975, hundreds of thousands of pig heart valves have been used to replace defective heart valves in humans. Cow heart valves have also been used since 1981.

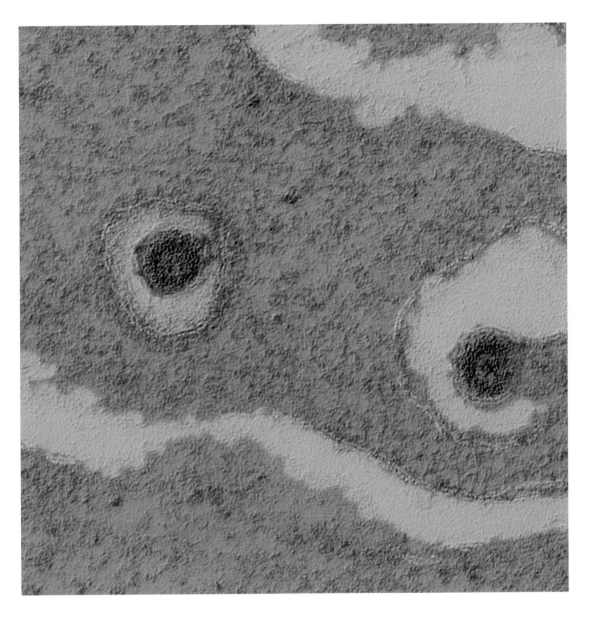

Genetic engineering to delete some specific pig genes and replace them with human genes may help to reduce the chances of rejection. Mixing the genes in this way would create a 'transgenic' animal, which would have both pig and human genes. However, there is much debate about whether xenotransplantation should be attempted at all. There is a risk that animal viruses may be transferred to humans. Also, the introduction of animal genes into the human gene pool may have long-term consequences that we cannot even imagine at the moment.

This micrograph shows a pig virus called porcine endogenous retrovirus (red) in the process of infecting a culture of human kidney cells (green). This virus does not harm pigs, but the discovery that it can infect human cells has led to concern that it might cause disease if pig organs are transplanted into humans.

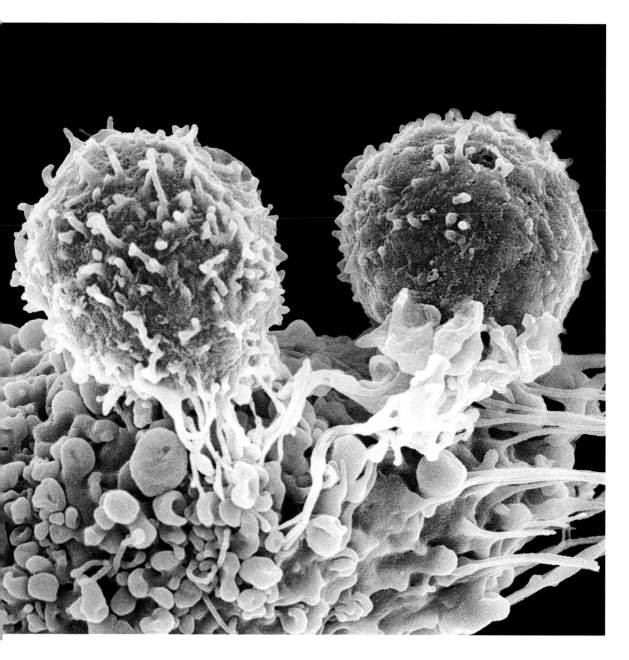

Induced tolerance

During the 1950s, a scientist called Ray Billingham, working in Oxford, UK, carried out similar research to Peter Medawar and Frank Macfarlane Burnet (see page 11) and proved that the immune system does not recognize things as 'foreign' immediately after birth. Experimenting on newborn mice, he transplanted skin from a black mouse onto the back of a white mouse. In older mice this

In this micrograph, white blood cells (orange) are seen attacking a 'foreign' cell (blue). This image has been magnified 4,000 times.

would have been rejected, but in newborn mice there was no rejection. He theorized that the immune system might learn to accept, or tolerate, the foreign tissue.

Recently, other scientists have returned to this idea. They have successfully transplanted organs in very young babies, even when the tissue types of the organ and baby do not match. Fetuses with life-threatening conditions have even been put on the transplant list before birth, and received a transplant – usually from other babies who have died – within a few hours of being born. The immature immune system does not recognize the transplant as foreign and so the baby tolerates the organ.

It has also been found that in older children and adults, giving the patient an infusion of bone marrow cells from the donor before a transplant reduces the risk of rejection. This is called 'induced tolerance' and it has been used successfully in some heart and kidney transplants. Research is continuing to find other methods of inducing tolerance, which would eliminate the need for the tissue type of the organ to match that of the recipient.

CUTTING EDGE — SCIENCE

The Human Genome Project

The genome of a species is the genetic code carried on the chromosomes in the nucleus (the cell's control centre) of every cell of an individual. After thirteen years of research, scientists from many different countries worked together and mapped the complete human genome in 2003. Scientists have used this information to develop some genetic tests which allow the very early detection of rejection by a simple blood test. Scientists also hope to be able to alter specific parts of the code, enabling the body to repair damage or prevent damage occurring, thus making organ transplantation unnecessary. By understanding more about the human genome, scientists will be better able to assess the implications of introducing animal genes into the human gene pool.

There are also likely to be many other ways in which our understanding of the human genome may be used to allow progress in the field of organ transplantation. These could include more accurate matching of donors and recipients; genetic engineering of animal cells to create organs that will not be rejected; and a greater understanding of the immune system and how it can be controlled.

Glossary

abdomen The part of the body between the pelvis and the chest that contains the stomach, intestines and other organs.

agglutinate Cause cells such as red blood cells to stick together in clumps.

antibody A chemical produced by the immune system in response to an antigen.

antigen A substance that the immune system recognizes as 'foreign'.

artery A blood vessel that carries blood away from the heart.

autograft A transplant using a person's own tissue, cells or fluid (also known as an isograft).

biopsy Removal of a small piece of tissue for examination.

bone marrow The tissue at the centre of some bones.

bronchoscopy Examination of the main airways using a tiny camera.

cartilage A fibrous tissue that cushions joints.

cell A tiny unit from which living things are made.

chemotherapy Chemical treatment of disease.

chromosome One of the chemical chains that carry the genetic information.

cornea The transparent layer at the front of the eye.

cryopreserve Preserve by freezing at a very low temperature.

CT scan (Computerised tomography) A type of X-ray that provides detailed, three-dimensional computer images of organs.

dialysis Filtering blood to remove waste chemicals.

donor A person who donates an organ, tissue, cells or fluid for a transplant.

echocardiogram A test of heart function using ultrasound echoes.

electrocardiogram (ECG) A test of the electrical activity of the heart.

gene A small part of a chromosome that carries the instructions for a particular feature.

genetic code The sequence of information carried by the full set of chromosomes.

genetic engineering Altering the genetic information of a cell.

genome The complete genetic code of an organism.

graft Another word for transplant.

graft-versus-host reaction An attack on a transplant patient's tissues by the immune system cells in a donor organ.

harvesting Removing an organ, fluid or tissue for transplantation, testing or research.

heart The organ that pumps blood around the body.

heart valve One of the flaps inside the heart that open and close to regulate blood flow.

heterograft A transplant between individuals of different species (also known as a xenograft).

homograft A transplant between individuals of same species (also known as an allograft).

hormone A chemical 'messenger' that travels through the blood to affect cells around the body.

immune system The body's defence system.

immunosuppress Prevent the immune system from working.

induced tolerance Non-rejection of an organ whose tissue type is different from the recipient's.

kidney An organ that filters blood to remove waste chemicals.

ligament A strong band of fibres that holds bones and cartilage in place.

liver An organ that carries out many functions, such as removal of toxins from blood.

lobe A rounded division of an organ, such as the brain or liver.

lungs Organs where oxygen enters the blood and carbon dioxide leaves the blood.

microsurgery Surgery using magnifying techniques and tiny instruments.

nucleus The part of a cell that contains the chromosomes and controls cell functions.

organ A group of tissues that work together.

pancreas An organ involved in controlling the level of sugar in the blood.

plasma The clear, liquid part of blood that blood cells float around in.

platelets Tiny cell fragments that help blood to clot.

radiotherapy Medical treatment using radiation such as X-rays and gamma rays.

rejection An attack by the immune system of a transplant recipient on a donor organ.

saline Containing salt.

semipermeable membrane A thin, flexible sheet that allows some types of particle to pass through, but not others.

spirometer Equipment that measures lung function and efficiency.

stem cell A cell that has the potential to develop into any other cell type.

syngeneic graft A transplant between genetically identical people.

system A group of organs that work together.

tendon A band of tissue that attaches a muscle to a bone or a muscle to another muscle.

tissue A group of similar cells that work together.

toxins Poisons produced by organisms, especially bacteria, which are capable of causing disease.

vein A blood vessel that carries blood to the heart.

ventricle A chamber of the heart.

X-ray An image of the body obtained by using a beam of radioactive waves.

Further Information

BOOKS

Body Focus: The Immune System by Carol Ballard (Heinemann Library, 2004)

21st Century Science: Medicine by Robin Kerrod (Franklin Watts, 2004)

Science at the Edge: Organ Transplantation by Anne Fullick (Heinemann Library, 2002)

Science Fact Files: The Human Body by John Farndon (Hodder Wayland, 2001)

Scalpels, Stitches and Scars: A History of Surgery by John Townsend (Raintree, 2005)

WEBSITES

www.uktransplant.org.uk
This website provides information about organ transplantation in the UK.

www.ustransplant.org
This website provides information about organ transplantation in the USA.

www.donors1.org
On this website you can find information about donating organs.

www.marrow.org
On this website you can find information about bone marrow donations.

www.transplantkids.co.uk
This website is about young people, their families and organ transplants.

Index